The Plural Space

The Plural Space

poems by Matthew Mahaney

This collection copyright © 2016 by Matthew Mahaney

All rights reserved. No part of this publication may be reproduced, stored in a retrieval system, rebound or transmitted in any form or by any means, electronic, mechanical, photocopying, recording or otherwise, without the prior written permission of the author and publisher. This book is sold subject to the condition that it shall not by way of trade or otherwise be lent, resold, hired out or otherwise circulated without the publisher's prior consent in any form of binding or cover other than that in which it is published.

Some of these poems appeared previously in the following journals: *Birdfeast, Gigantic Sequins, ILK, Inter|rupture, Salt Hill, Skydeer Helpking, Wildness.*

ISBN number: 978-0-9933508-3-2

Printed and Bound by 4edge Limited

Cover design by Matthew Korbel-Bowers

Typeset by Andrew Hook

Published by:
Salò Press
85 Gertrude Road
Norwich
UK

editorsalòpress@gmail.com
www.salòpress.weebly.com

The Plural Space is Eerie rhythm exploring a density, an expansiveness that surrounds you so closely you blur or speak. This book is a layered / precise glance at Sound created by body or machine / at Sound as it hangs between / as it travels between those who use it to communicate / commune / those who struggle with its complex presence. Do you listen / Do you watch it. How can bewilderment be calm. Darkening water? How can sound and speech and listening distort shape / nature / sentence? The gathering thickness of these poems is terrifying and necessary, totally blood filled and churning / a ribboning and beautiful space.

   - Carrie Lorig, author of *The Pulp vs. The Throne*

In *The Plural Space*, the world's dispersed elements compose a drifting grid. Here, the reconfigured vocabularies of botany, physics, human emotion, and animal intelligence generate a hypnotic feedback loop. Matthew Mahaney has recorded the acoustics of an ever-expanding room.

   - Eric Baus, author of *The Tranquilized Tongue*

THE PLURAL SPACE
Warm Fawn	3
Harmed Swan	4
Ash Farm	5
Pearl Swarm	6
Frozen Grass	7
Cell Song	8
Water Order	9

BACKGROUND VOICES
Snow Echoes	13
A Memory at the Cellular Level	14
Orchid Corners	15
The Actual Echo Failed to Appear	16
Recording the Memory Version	17
Quartz Lung	18
Muted Limbs	19
Stuttered Sulfer	20

THE LISTENING MACHINES
Static Blooms	25
Tracking the Dislocated Echo	26
Sleep Help	27
To Think About Speech	28
Passive Magnets	29
The Pearl Sound	30
The Lives of a Sentence	31
Ice Wrapped in Paper	32
Machine Noise	38
Sleep Sounds	39
Small Senses	40
Noise Weight	41
Fox Expression	42
Paper Snow	43

Memory Static — 44
Glass Hiss — 45
The Illness Spreads Like Coral — 46
Music Exposure — 47

SPEECH MEMORIES — 49

FALSE SOUNDS
Machine Mother — 63
How Sounds are Made — 64
Opaque Coughs — 65

THE PLURAL SPACE

WARM FAWN

In the plural space, machines
are taught

to mimic
how a skeleton unbuckles.

An animal dismantles. Softly, each
taxonomy undoes its seamless structure.

There is a splash before the final absence.
A small impression steams from some new corner of a cloud.

Can an orchid simply ossify?

                      How an organ floats.
                      How unflattering.

HARMED SWAN

A harmed swan wears its wound on the left. When it sweeps the lake red, it is facing west. Its strain clones an axe-maker's music. Pinched silk in the sleeve of my ear.

ASH FARM

The ash farm unfastens its fence.
Soon the soil has hatched a litter.

Each in its own
channel unfurls

and flexes. Their chatter
makes an almost-message.

A bat's eye viewed.
Seeds pressed black in forest light.

PEARL SWARM

A creature swims in injured water.
It helps itself to illness.

Unseen ducts secrete a kind of silk performed
by chemicals.

They pulse in steady intervals.

Soon its seams will spill a quantity of milk.

This is all to do with infestation.
With fixation.

The sound is of an opening. It is
an opera of orifice.

FROZEN GRASS

A wandering unsteadies itself as the cold works
a window to save its shape.

Two thin molecules uncurl and we clench our teeth
in unison.

Outside an aphid winces as a frost spirals in.

The grass iced-over tangles.
It makes a water altar is one thing I was thinking.

Dead aphids feel like ice is another.

                                        This is wrong.
                                        They float like ice.

CELL SONG

An unborn aphid defrosts beneath the soil. Its green not-blood confuses several seeds. In the time it takes the cadence of their sprouting to echo in the rain, an orchid's cells can be cloned.

WATER ORDER

An exoskeleton is awash in unwanted ions.
Water presses hard against a dying cell's wall.

                              It permeates.

A necessary presence.
A known percentage.
An organ

      subsists on what it's made of.

In this way, a forest or a jungle or a polar ice cap is not so different from our own warm bodies.

BACKGROUND VOICES

SNOW ECHOES

Some of us have been assigned to the plural space.
We search for stray speech.

An accident.
An occupation.

There are rumors that the vowels look like ghosts.
When an unexpected echo forms, it swells metallic and heavy.

There is a warming of the inner ear.
An undercurrent's voltage.

Two funerals commence in the interval. The time it takes to calculate the distance between listeners.

A MEMORY AT THE CELLULAR LEVEL

An iris cloud sings static. It separates its echo into slow and cotton, then sinks to further sleep. It wakes in the shape of a tentacle. In an unperformed memory, sea urchins swell. When an undercurrent grazes their shells, they remember cell division. The salt it makes. How their yellow meat mists.

ORCHID CORNERS

An unnamed shape reminded me of the background voice.
I trained an eye:
                this is snow.
                This is how an owl curves.

In the time it takes a cloud to house
an echo, a cell began
to suffocate.

An attic bloomed.
Each warm corner blinked an orchid.

THE ACTUAL ECHO FAILED TO APPEAR

Something orange occurred, reminding me of speech. The trees refused to shade or didn't hear us ask. I tried to remember the way a listener looks.

How an answer tends to follow.

RECORDING THE MEMORY VERSION

Everyone was in agreement. I performed the background voice without incident while the others combed their owls. For the memory version of the evening we each produced a single stutter. We wanted something guttural. A communal error for the echo to embrace.

QUARTZ LUNG

By exhaling in unison, we grew our breath in crystals.
We blew a glass throat.

Our vowels spread like static in the plural space.

Their hollows twinned.
Their ions echoed red.

This was when we learned
the oxygen in snow can be used to summon speech.

This was when we started sleeping in the memory room.

MUTED LIMBS

A whisper echoed wet caves.

I pressed my knuckles. I crawled
a carpal tunnel. At its exit

I saw the corners of my body
in purple and gravel.

I could see my words were going
numb, so I kept my mouth shut.
My senses clicking.

To keep a forward face.
I stepped a jagged line out.

Three times is more than I remember but each one felt
so feral and damp.

STUTTERED SULFUR

I found a dormant echo in the gap of a conversation. Its slope incurred a system based on overlapping graphs. Somewhere in the space between noticing and appreciating, a strain of stray speech materialized. It started when it saw the echo, but the warmth of my mouth kept it distracted. It shuddered in and out of order, then pulled itself into a language posture.

THE LISTENING MACHINES

STATIC BLOOMS

The machines look like wasps.

When their legs are right
angles, everyone can see
that I am listening.

Static blooms in long pauses.

I often wonder if I have ever been
an unintended listener.

TRACKING THE DISLOCATED ECHO

Frost finds an aphid's wing and the machines
release an unintended song.

Its pitch is paper. It echoes
wrong.

As the echo travels
milky cables, the machines
grow steam.

I search my pockets for pink wing fragments.
I taste a pill's ink.

The seeds I scatter on the snow perform
my only memory of a map.

SLEEP HELP

When the machines are awake, every blink is a thunderclap. An airport smell attaches itself to my skin and I search for purple holes to fall into. Since the machines arrived, sleep only comes with help. With my face clouded. With towels and alcohol. My placid all out of place.

TO THINK ABOUT SPEECH

A small girl draws a mountain range in crayon. Her brother finds it later and draws two airplanes firing dotted lines against the bottom of the page.

This is how to think about speech.

An echo lives in the space between dots, in the discord of letters uncomfortably paired. When a sentence unfolds across adequate space, its shape is maintained, its timbre unharmed. In the event of resistance, a sentence will surrender its vowels.

The stray speech that lives in the plural space is an example of this.

PASSIVE MAGNETS

A cloud remembers red.
It strains against its shape until it scatters

salt and static. We walk beneath
the curled oval an owl makes.

When we find a river
we don't remember, we seed it
with stones.

We mourn the passive magnets the owl eyes became.
A speech is made, though no one thinks to echo.

I blame the silk
we cough
for weeks on the machines.

THE PEARL SOUND

The plural space fills with white static.

Has the algorithm for wind noise changed?
Is the static truly white?

Someone says *the pearl sound*.

Their hands are making seeds. The machines
have been exposed to snow and
their hands are making seeds.

This is not the pearl sound.

The way a needle seals a wound.
How stray speech infects an open window.

THE LIVES OF A SENTENCE

Sentences read and write in different ways, and understand very little about either process. Many sentences spend their entire lives unwritten. Even more write only once, and subsequently read only once, or perhaps a handful of times if they are lucky.

Sentences envy their words for their ability to write, read, and speak without any need for them. The words never know this, however, having never known any other way of life.

Colonialism is a popular Halloween costume in Western Canada is a sentence that wishes it would be written more often. *Fasten with adhesive mixed with vinegar and ice* is another, though it would like to speak even more.

ICE WRAPPED IN PAPER

Every six days, she comes to put the machines to sleep. She presses her thumbs against each corner until the cables sweat milk. After this, the static stops.

When the machines are asleep, I remember ice.

I remember what it sounded like
not stepping on paper.

I wonder what would happen if she stopped visiting and does she think the word *mother* when she presses her thumbs? Does she know when the machines will learn the difference between noise and sound?

There is always an orange chime before they wake.
It never echoes.

When the machines wake up, they are dry.

Their cables run clear and I can tell
they have learned a new set of shapes to imitate.

She leaves, but I don't notice her hair.

I am listening too much.

MACHINE NOISE

Every morning the machines inspect themselves.
They cannot not do this.

Their cables unbraid. They blur into
glass and something red

spins in my ears. Whenever this happens, we speak
miles of wire beneath inches of wax.

She tells me to imagine a moth.
The amplified void it swims in the bowl of a lamp.

SLEEP SOUNDS

I cannot ignore the transit within my body. I have had to stop lying on my side. As if designed to do so, the machines conduct the steady flicker in my neck, the metronomic hell forever spilling from my ear.

SMALL SENSES

A static shadow

collapses.

The red fog of its sound
cups my ears
in a loving way, and an alphabet
reverses.

The vibration this releases
breeds a hive
and my tongue

recalls the wasp
a machine resembles.

NOISE WEIGHT

The machines are always searching for sound. I'm tired of waking up every morning with their weight behind my ears. When the wind hits, their cables swell and drink their fill. The static this creates is darker than expected. We keep our hands in our pockets. We remind each other of moths.

FOX EXPRESSION

She is speaking orange steam.

She makes a fox expression and I experience
a new range of heat. An unbreathing pause wrapped
around us like cotton.

The steam tastes like salt.
It makes me speech-tired.

I am already used to all of this:

>the seeds in my pocket,
>her pearled tongue,
>the embryonic echoes taking shape between
>my teeth.

PAPER SNOW

One of the machines is sick.

Its chime is colorless. It coughs
fogged glass.

Can an unintended orifice be a symptom?

Is it better if it snows
burnt paper or ash?

Ten grains of rice form a letter in my fist.

Someone is looking
for their telephone voice.

She monitors the neutral music as it covers her.

I watch all of this through the echoed rain, through
the pink milk ice that clings
to every corner of the diseased machine.

MEMORY STATIC

When I reach the fence, I can see that I have not been listening. The machines are still making dead leaves. To drown it out, I close my eyes and make a metal sound until my teeth begin to separate. All of us are lying about the ash in our pockets. The clouds slow down, then steam. The memory static we talk about afterward is real.

GLASS HISS

The word *artifact* clicks in my mouth in a tentative way. My tongue curls but before I can speak it is gone. It diffuses into roots and stems and a dark string of others exits instead. The machines flex their gills greedily. Despite being built for the plural space, they have started ignoring its pattern of glass. They seek thickets of pitches.

THE ILLNESS SPREADS LIKE CORAL

The sick machine is dying.
It bleats a skeletal song.

A pink salt shadow
spans the length of one leg.

She has to visit on the wrong day.

When she disconnects the fattest cable, everyone hears
the milk it births. The vein of ice
it opens clouds

my ears until I find a cough
and drop
a magnet down its throat.

She calms the machine with private patterns.

She cleans it with snow.

MUSIC EXPOSURE

We are surrounded by machines.

Feed them, she says.

There is grass woven tightly around each of my fingers.
There is moss and there are aphids dying.
Their wings dissolve in pink
and yellow traces.

Still there are the machines.

I want to ask her why, but a layer of music is
unfolding from her eyes.
It coats my tongue like the pollen a wasp wears.

I knew this was coming, I think.

SPEECH MEMORIES

I write words to hear their echo. I watch them breathe through their vowels. The mist that this produces will often land on other pages, just as bones can sometimes wander through the body like a boat.

A room records the conversation it creates. If this recording finds an open window, a speech memory must be made.

An echo is a kind of record, an unplanned documentation of speech. If I accept that an echo is a kind of ghost, and that one form of *ghost* is an unwanted memory, it can be said that an entry into record-keeping has been found.

An echo must remember. To say an echo is a kind of speech memory would be incorrect, though an echo can be changed.

If a memory outlives its owner, questions are asked. Is the memory speech-related? Has its echo found an heir? Other potential scenarios may include photographs of trees beneath mattresses, an undated letter in the corner of your eye. To put it another way, what does a funeral record?

The first step in assessing speech memories is to search the room for animal fibers. This is not to say that buildings of a feral architecture will be any more conducive to the creation or housing of speech memories. Domestic interiors will always have their own special barriers and access points.

To convert an echo into a speech memory requires the proper coding. The conversion rate of wind plays a role. Or in its absence, rust.

With my hands hidden, I found a speech memory. It was buried in the background voice. I wondered what kind of listener was intended. In the time it takes an echo's color to collapse, the room began to molt. I forgot to close the windows. I forgot about my hands.

FALSE SOUNDS

MACHINE MOTHER

She warns me that ice will begin growing, but I already know this. *Soon it will sound like a gunshot*, I say. She answers with snow but I am not a machine. I ask her why the water I drink sounds metallic, where the space between listening and hearing lies. At night I listen to the background voices. I remember how her face looked when she asked if I was sure.

HOW SOUNDS ARE MADE

She tried to help the machines sleep but only made their music brighter. There was wind but the volume was off.

Then she was saying could I hear her and how did I feel while her hands drew snow and dirt on my cheek. Her knees were red from kneeling in the snow. She pulled a piece of paper from her pocket that said *intestinal braiding*.

I listened to her using her sympathy voice.

When I opened my eyes again, I could feel the orange chimes. Their echoes were thick in the milk of my body.

OPAQUE COUGHS

Each time I cough I expect to hear new leaves being made into paper, but instead there are bells.

Bells sweating rust.

Bells soaked in bloody wool.

Bells dripping
honey
in the palm of my hand.

She offers me the damp sleeve of her voice, but my throat
has succumbed to the dust
my lungs found.

                                                Digital dust.
                                                Actual dust.

My coughs grow opaque.
The soft white smoke at the center of ice.

I watch her watching me, wondering what a higher pitch signifies, whether the arc of a wave forms an atonal glare.

She amends her notes.

She grafts her voice to the falling light.

Her music marks the room's borders. It stirs
a wasp's corpse.

It is hard to stop watching the patterns she makes. Even before I begin searching for the wandering song my dust-lungs lost, I know I won't be able to find it.

I know I won't remember the bells.

Matthew Mahaney is the author of *Your Attraction to Sharp Machines* (BatCat Press, 2013) and *The Storm that Bears Your Name* (The Cupboard, 2015). He lives in Madison, Wisconsin.